Ypres

April 22nd 1915

The first gas attack

Yves Buffetaut
Translated by Catherine Cook

"Un Jour de la Grande Guerre"

YSEC

THE FRENCH ARMIES AT YPRES, FROM OCTOBER 1914 TO APRIL 1915

After the setback on the Marne, and the stabilisation of the front on the river Aisne, the German and Allied armies tried to leapfrog each other by heading north, in what was called "The Race to the Sea".

Naturally, this race, which brought no tangible result, finished in Belgium. By mid-October almost the entire kingdom was in the hands of the Germans and, because of the floods created by the Belgians, the only sector that could support a large scale attack was the region around Ypres. By October 23rd 1914 the front had stabilised and formed a distinctive bulge around the old woollen town, going from Armentieres to Gheluvelt and Zonnebeke in the west, before heading north in the region of Bixschoote. The British Expeditionary Force took up positions around Ypres, from Armentieres to Zonnebeke, whilst the Belgian detachment of the French army held the northern front of Ypres, flanked by the Belgian army. On the German side the whole front was held by the 4th Army consisting of four regular army Korps.

The Kaiser enters the fray.

Realising that the war of mobility had ground to a halt in the sands of Flanders, the German High Command attempted a break through at Ypres in order to march on Calais and thus directly threaten the southern coast of England. The plan was audacious, as demonstrated by the presence of the Kaiser himself on the battlefield near Thielt. The attack started on October 29th 1914 with particular robustness. The Michelin guide to Ypres, written immediately after the war and showing

Ypres' Great Square with, in the background, the famous Cloth Hall and the cathedral. This scene takes place in October 1914, at the time when British troops arrive. Vehicles are parked in the square next to a Field Hospital. (IWM Q 57285)

Ypres' Great Square, April 1915, just before the German attack. On the left, the front of the Hall is still standing but many houses have been hit and some have collapsed. (IWM Q 61614)

5

no sympathy for the Germans, notes that "up until November 15th, German regiments, spurred on by the presence of their Emperor, threw themselves against the Ypres salient with incredible frenzy and with little regard for casualties". We do not intend to describe in detail the events of the first battle of Ypres, but it is nevertheless necessary to summarise it in order to better understand future developments. German pressure across the whole of the Ypres front was so powerful that, on the night of October 31st, the Allied line was forced back in all areas. In the central sector Zonnebeke was lost but Gheluvelt held fast. On the other hand, in the south-east, the Germans made significant advances. The village of Messines was the scene of a particularly fierce struggle, from October 30th to November 1st, on which date it fell to the Germans. The same day, they also took the neighbouring village of Wytschaete, which opened a breach in the English lines. At this point Maréchal French ordered a withdrawal, but Foch, who commanded the northern armies, immediately counter-manded his decision: "Maréchal, we must hold, hold at all costs. Hold until tonight, I'm coming to help". And Foch did not hesitate to call in "Wellington's old infantry" which enabled him to convince French.

Some Zouaves (Algerian infantry fighting in discreet units as part of the French Army) were sent into battle to fight alongside the British. Together they held Saint-Eloi, north of Wytshaete, but only managed to slow the enemy. It took the intervention of the 14th French Corps in this sector, and as far as Messines, to consolidate, momentarily, Allied positions. On November 11th 1914 the Germans renewed their attack with great vigour. Allied forces gave way across the whole front and in some areas German elite Guards regiments move forward four kilometres in a terrifying wave. The British counter-attacked, which enabled them to slow down the Germans and to re-establish a front line just a few kilometres away from the city walls. The front was stabilised over the next few days on a line that ran from the west of Messines to the outskirts of Wytschaete, then on to Saint-Eloi, passing by Hill 60 and the eastern suburbs of Zillebeke to Hooge, then Saint-Julien and Langemark. It was during attacks on this part of the front that German forces, recruited from student bodies, literally drowned in their own blood as they tried to breach the front in celebration of the Kaiser's birthday, their unquestionable bravery not compensating for their lack of experience.

Scottish soldiers in a trench set up beside a ruined farm near Ypres. The ground is so waterlogged that it is often impossible to dig trenches: they have to be made with sandbags. (Ysec collection)

The front line is defined.

The end of the attack did not mean the end of the fighting and all is not quiet on the Ypres front. December 17th 1914, Langemark and Bixschoote were captured by the Germans. The same day the French attacked in the area of Steenstraate, to the north. This date is important as it is the date of a major offensive launched by Maréchal Joffre which turns into a

The caption from the time says only that this is Ypres Hospital on the Great Square. The picture was taken in April 1915 and the presence of dead horses shows that the area was frequently under German artillery fire. (IWM Q 61631)

French and English cavalry at Ypres, October 1914. It is impossible to identify the English cavalry, but the French rider on the left wears a helmet of the heavy cavalry, that is to say the armoured cavalry or the dragoons. (IWM Q 60700)

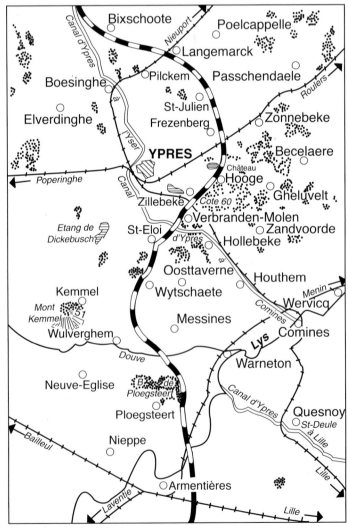

Map : Belgian front after the first battle at Ypres.

terrible fiasco. Claude Prieur, a naval infantry officer, wrote in his diary on that date: "English ambulances brought a large number of casualties to Oostvleteren. The Geynet battalion (1 company of the 1st battalion) and a part of the Mauros battalion (3 company of the 2nd battalion) launched a partial attack this morning the other side of Streenstraate bridge. Despite capturing three machine guns and a section of trench, despite a few German prisoners (earlier, one of them in passing said, in excellent French, "well done the marines, you did really well"), the results do not seem marvellous and losses were heavy. Captain Geynet, who charged at the head of his men, is missing; a naval lieutenant, an ensign, and two company officers were killed (…)"The day after, Prieur wrote: "The last of the attack's casualties, including lieutenant Bonelli, finished arriving. Most of them must have stayed for hours, or even the whole day, in the mud and water. Beware of gas gangrene! Few people were hit by artillery shells; almost all that I saw had been hit by bullets". On December 20th 1914, Prieur visited the captured territory: "hardly exceptional, this patch of ground that our marines took on the 17th: for a trench, a rectangular ditch, where men endeavour to bail out the muddy water with their mess tins. The parapet is far from solid. To cap it all, the rain is falling without mercy once

Franse lichte cavalerie
Some French light cavalry
take a halt on the outskirts
of Ypres, October 1914. On
the horse, in the fore ground,
we can make out a lance.
(IWM Q 60711)

more and my sailors have neither tarpaulins, nor waterproof sleeping bags. Many no longer have wool blankets, lost in some previous fight". Prieur, whose rudimentary shelter is so low that he cannot sit up straight, and so short that he cannot comfortably lay down, is reduced to staying "huddled on a bucket- lid which still does not stop the water from coming up "usque ad intima"... When he observed the German lines, the picture was even worse: "Between us, some old trenches full of corpses; and to top it all, at the foot of the enemy's barbed wire entanglements, a sad row of marines, in positions of crawling infantry, frozen in death after their assault was wiped out by machine-gun fire".

The weather does not favour widespread operations, as noted a French colonel: "The land we are fighting on is awful: the crust of 30 centimetres is relatively good, but underneath it is mud and even more mud. Men stuck in 'des boyaux', or trenches, of one metre or one and a half metres deep, get sucked deeper and deeper into the mud until many hands are needed to pull them out".

On December 24th, Prieur complains of the effect the bad weather is having on his men: "That's it. My NCO was right: 70 men, just from my company, reported sick. How will the two battalion doctors be able to examine all that lot, sort out the sick from the malingerers who would be happy to spend a few days in the warm, whilst the others return to

A French front line trench in March 1915, when part of the French front had been entrusted to the British. The latter subsequently complained about the bad state of the trenches they received. In this picture we see that the trench was built above ground (and not dug out for reasons already mentioned) is missing a parados and offers relative little shelter. (IWM Q 61595)

the quagmire? Few frozen feet, apparently, but rheumatism, chilblains and diarrhoea".

Doctor Nel, in his book, rich in documented detail (Boesinghe, or the battles of the 87th Territorial Division on the Yser), describes the Division's return to the Boesinghe section, north of Ypres, on January 30th 1915 : "It is no longer the all-out struggle to take possession of enemy ground, it is the guarding of trenches, 80 metres from the Germans, with daily losses by bullet and shell. It's the interminable winter in the mud, with the appearance of cases of frozen feet, the evacuation of typhoid sufferers. After such miserable times March gives way to a sunny spring which transforms the scenery. Life becomes more bearable and better organisation improves our existence".

Prieur also noted an improvement at the end of December, not without a certain sense of humour: "Sunday 27th December (…) To provide themselves with shelter our men scour the ground between the lines at night, scavenging German tarpaulins, an article in great demand by the marines (…) Monday 28th December. Little by little we are getting issued with all the latest equipment: first we received star shell rockets, followed by hand grenades. This evening, our tireless Colonel takes it upon himself to install a telephone line up to the front. The smallest umbrella would do for me. The downpour has become so violent, with its accompanying gales, that everything is soaked through. My hovel is a swamp (…). The hunt for tarpaulins continues. They brought us some sheets of tar paper to make roofs: we have to fight with the more resourceful of our men to stop them from cutting it into individual strips".

And so the war of the trenches sets in, with its procession of small miseries, due mainly to the condition of the ground and the continual damp. Of course, shells and occasional sniper fire bring a few losses, but it is mainly the evacuation of the sick which brings down numbers. Inexorably, the position of the front line is defined. Doctor Nel, in his book, gives a highly detailed description of the different positions, trenches and 87th Territorial Division strongholds from Steenstraat to Langemarck. We cannot quote here the details, which cover over two pages, but we have reproduced the map he drew up with his own hand and which is of great interest. It has been reproduced in it's entirety by us and is the only precise map of the French front available today. This whole front, from the front line to the Yser canal, will be captured by the Germans on April 22nd 1915.

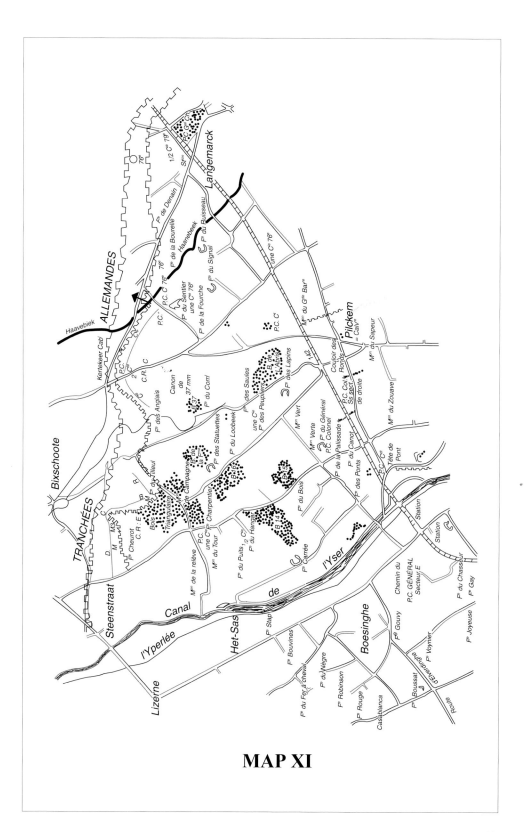

MAP XI

13

THE GERMAN PLAN
AND THE PREPARATIONS
FOR BATTLE

(Page 14-15) The cloud of gas on April 22nd 1915 was created by the emission of chlorine from cylinders but it seems that gas shells were also used during the second battle of Ypres. In any case, gas shells were widely used during the following years because they were not dependent on winds: lobbed into the valley bottoms, and especially on enemy artillery positions and communication routes, they were able to isolate entire sections of the front. This 210 mm howitzer was pictured in 1915, but there are no clues as to where the picture was taken. (IWM Q 55019)

T he use of gas by the Germans has been the subject of much controversy from its first use in April 1915 and time has not calmed the debate. According to the Reich's records the Germans never intended the possible use of suffocating gas prior to the war but, from the month of October 1914, everything changed. First of all, there were rumours that the French had invented a secret weapon, Turpinite, capable of killing men without causing any visible wounds. This was widely reported in the Allied press and Octave Béliard, battalion doctor of the 66th Infantry Regiment, who will witness the first gas attack, cannot help but note after the battle: "We had taken a few dozen prisoners,

A large wooden bunker built in the German sector of western Flanders on the front facing Ypres. It is actually a farm covered in tree trunks to fortify it. As in the Allied sector, it was not possible to dig deeply because of the waterlogged nature of the soil. (Ysec collection)

including an officer who we had violently berated, criticising his nation's use of poison gas, contrary to the laws of war between two civilised nations (…). The prisoner showed unfeigned surprise: "What" he said, "you blame us for that, even when it was you who started it?" –"You lie!" we answered – "I am your prisoner", retorted proudly the officer, "and I don't give a damn about your insults. Kill me if you will, but do not insult me. I told the truth". This man was evidently telling the truth and his confidence troubled me. I was certain of our complete innocence but, thinking back to that conversation, I was always convinced that by spreading the false rumour of a knock-out powder, that Turpin had never in

A gas cylinder battery in the act of releasing its deadly cloud. The inconvenience of such a system is obvious: the gas cloud is totally at the mercy of the wind. For the Germans who, in general, were facing into the prevailing winds, this was a major handicap. This photograph, taken on an American training area at Chaumont in October 1918, demonstrates another shortcoming of this type of weapon: a large number of gas cylinders are necessary to create a cloud dense enough to be lethal.
(IWM Q 113282)

fact invented, our boffins hadn't helped us. It is quite likely that this false rumor will come back to haunt us."

The existence, real or imagined, of Turpinite was not a sufficient reason for the Germans to use gas. It rather seems that it was tactical considerations which were essential to their choice. The stabilisation of the front made it difficult to capture enemy positions, and each side was looking to find a way of returning to a war of mobility. But they still had to breech the front. To achieve that, the enemy had to be weakened by adequate preparation. Because of the closeness of the lines artillery fire was dangerous to friendly troops and the idea of sending over a cloud of gas, spreading everywhere, appeared promising. The gas, drifting into the dug-outs, would force the men to evacuate which would then make them easy targets.

Gas and The Hague Convention

The Hague Conventions, dating from July 29th 1899 and October 18th 1907, laid down the laws of war. Both of them forbade the use of suffocating gases without, however, indicating what measures would be taken against the country that used them. Nor did they arrive at an exact definition of a suffocating gas. The Germans first experimented with an irritating gas, a sort of sneezing powder, which was placed in shrapnel shells, the weapon being named the "Niespulver".

The Allies condemn the use of gas by the Germans as soon as they are a victim of it, but immediately started to produce some for themselves as well. We can see here French soldiers in front of a system for diffusing gas: many containers are linked together by a pipe onto a gallery which allows the concentration of the gas emissions. Note that none of the French soldiers visible in this picture are wearing gas masks. (Ysec collection)

This system was used from October 27th 1914, when 3,000 shells of this type were fired against Indian and British troops in the Neuve-Chapelle sector. The results were not very impressive as the Niespulver seemed to cause no discomfort at all to the Allied troops. Following this failure the Germans put together another shell, the T-Granate, named after its inventor, the chemist Hans Tappen. This time the weapon was used against the Russians, in January 1915, but because of the extreme cold the irritating gas revealed itself to be completely useless.

From itching powder to suffocating gas

During the winter of 1914-1915 Professor Doktor Fritz Haber worked on the possibility of enveloping enemy lines under a cloud of gas released from high pressure cylinders using the wind to push the gas cloud up to the enemy trenches. The gas proposed by Haber was liquid chlorine which, on being released from cylinders, forms a volatile cloud: the interesting point is that it spreads slowly enough to gas the enemy infantry but it also disperses fast enough to allow the German infantry to follow-up quickly and capture the enemy positions.

Haber's proposal was accepted and liquid chlorine was immediately put into production by domestic German industry which prevented suspicions being aroused. At the same time the first gas masks were tested.

The choice of the test battlefield

According to official German records tests of the new secret weapon were already so far advanced by this time that

General von Falkenhayn decided to try it out on a battlefield. The only vector of the gas is the wind, which was quite a problem as the prevailing wind in France is essentially western. However, meteorologists demonstrated that, in Flanders, the wind is often from the south in spring. The only part of the front where the German lines faced north was on the southern outskirts of Ypres, in the sector controlled by the 15th Army Korps. On January 25th General von Deimling, who commanded this Korps, was ordered to report to German GHQ at Charleville-Mézières. Falkenhayn tells him that his sector had been chosen to test the gas. Deimling asked for a large quantity of gas, to be sure to be able to make a significant breakthrough. Falkenhayn refused under the pretext that he only wanted to carry out a test. It was only to be a question of improving the first line positions.

For this full scale test 6,000 cylinders were sent to Flanders and were given the name of "F batteries", whereas the cloud of gas received the code name of "Disinfection". But the wind proved to be unpredictable: it never blew in the desired direction, which prevented any experiments. Furthermore, many German officers were opposed to the

German trenches in the Ypres sector, 1915. The ground has not yet been churned up by artillery fire. (Ysec collection)

A general view of Ypres, April 1915. Compared to pictures in the previous chapter, the destruction is more significant: the roof of the Hall has collapsed, as has that of the cathedral, the belfry and the steeple have received a number of hits and the side wall of the Hall has fallen in. (IWM Q 61646)

use of gas, some of them for moral reasons, others for reasons of operational efficiency. Some of them were scared for the lives of their own men; others, beginning with Crown Prince Rupprecht of Bavaria, were afraid because they thought that the weapon would be turned against the German empire, simply because the prevailing winds were from the west and so the Allies would have a lot more opportunity to use it than the Germans.

An offensive against Ypres

From mid-March the Germans actively prepared a major offensive at Ypres, with the objective of breaching the salient and so encircling the Allied troops. It does not appear that the use of gas was an important element of the offensive due to the difficulties encountered with its use. In March the commander of the 4th Army, the Duke of Albrecht, decided to study another sector for the use of gas. On March 28th 1915 he chose the sector occupied by the 46th Reserve Division and the 26th Reserve Korps, stretching the six kilometres from Steenstraat, on the Yser canal, to Poelcapelle.

On April 5th Oberts Peterson and his unit of specialist engineers started to bury gas cylinders in the sector. The work lasted six days but, by April 11th, the new weapon was in place. No less than 5,730 cylinders had been buried in batteries of 20. In all, it would be possible to release 180,000

kilograms of chlorine in five minutes, constituting a lethal cloud.

The real goal of the German High Command

The objective of General von Falkenhayn remains a mystery more than 80 years after the battle, just as those of the battle of Verdun the year after. It seems that Falkenhayn had a strong propensity to justify his defeats for history by limiting the supposed extent of his offensives. Even more so than at Verdun, it seems impossible to know if, at Ypres, he was attempting a large scale offensive or not. Was Ypres the objective or was it simply the test of a new weapon?

Falkenhayn wrote after the battle that he had never intended to capture Ypres but only wanted to test the gas. However, the determination to continue the battle for many weeks after the initial success of April 22nd suggests that the Germans did want to take Ypres and reduce the salient. Therefore, at the beginning of April, the German troops prepared themselves for a limited offensive and not just a simple test. The words of General von Deimling, who commanded the 15th Army Korps facing Ypres, speak volumes: "On January 25th 1915 I was called to GHQ at Mézières with my Chiefs of Staff to confer with Falkenhayn. He made us aware that we were going to put into service a new war weapon, toxic gas, and that they were considering carrying out the first tests in my sector. The toxic gas would be delivered in steel cylinders which we would install in the trenches and which would be released as soon as the winds were favourable. I must admit that the idea of poisoning the enemy in the same way as we poison rats affected me as it would any honest soldier: it disgusted me. But if these toxic gases could bring about the fall of Ypres then maybe we could win a victory that would decide the fate of the whole campaign. Faced with such an enormous challenge we had to shut out our personal objections"

The fall of Ypres is commonly designated as the ultimate objective and which could even prefigure a larger victory. But, unbeknown to Deimling, this larger victory was not on the agenda for the western front. Falkenhayn only wanted to stop the western Allies from acting offensively in the west, preventing them from taking the initiative. His war objectives for 1915 were to gain a decisive victory in the east, thus releasing fresh troops for the western front the following year once the Russians have been defeated. We can therefore summarise Flakenhayn's different objectives for 1915 as follows:

1. Beat the Russians,

2. Prevent the Allies advancing in the west,

achieving those objectives by the following means:

1. Transfer some divisions to the east,

2. Hit Ypres with enough strength to disorganise the French and British armies.

This explains why the battle in Belgium lasted until the middle of May. Considering the battle of Ypres simply as an opportunity to test a new weapon makes no sense because the

facts clearly deny such an assertion. By striking at the interface of the French and British armies Falkenhayn was guaranteed to provoke the greatest possible confusion amongst the Allies.

A German NCO and his men in a trench on the Flanders front. The NCO is showing the photographer what allows the men to stand firm despite the damp: large wooden clogs full of hay. (IWM Q 51079)

The German plan in detail

On April 14th 1915 the 4th Army issued orders "for an attack on Pilckem ridge". According to these orders, the capture of Pilckem ridge would force the enemy to abandon the Ypres salient. Elsewhere, the second objective of the German troops was to dig in on the Yser canal up to and including Ypres. The principle objectives of the committed units were the following:

- 45th Reserve Division: to capture Steenstraat-Lizerne,
- 46th Reserve Division: to capture Lizerne-Het Sas-Pilckem,
- 26th Reserve Korps: to capture Pilckem ridge and the road running through Boesinghe-Pilckem-Langemarck-Poelcapelle.

The infantry were to attack with bayonets fixed but with rifles unloaded, as it was expected that the gas would have annihilated the enemy units. The attack was planned for April 15th... if the wind permitted.

The Allies warned of a gas attack

Many events which took place during the week before the German attack should have alerted the Allies. First of all, a German soldier deserted by surrendering to the French of General Ferry's 11th division. His name was August Jaeger, of the 234th Reserve Infantry Regiment (51st Reserve Division). Brought in by the 4th battalion, he was interrogated at the division's headquarters. He immediately provided considerable detail concerning the organisation of the German lines. He explained that the Germans were about to launch an offensive with the help of gas. General Mordacq, who was to have a major role in the battle as Colonel commanding the 90th Infantry Brigade quotes the words of Jaeger in his book "The Drama of the Yser", published in 1933,: "an imminent attack is being prepared against the French trenches. To support the attack four batteries of twenty cylinders of suffocating gas per company have been stocked in the front line trenches; each battery is operated by five men. At a given signal, three red rockets launched by the artillery, the cylinders are to be opened and the released gas is to be carried by a favourable wind towards the French trenches. This gas is supposed to suffocate the men occupying these trenches and allow the Germans to occupy them without any losses. So as not to be suffocated in turn, each man has an oxygen-impregnated rag". Jaeger thus confides to the interrogating officer the existence of a prototype gas mask.

After having read Jaeger's interrogation report General Ferry warned his superiors and took direct measures himself to protect his troops, in particular by reducing the number of men on the front line. He also warned his neighbours, the 28th Division and the 1st Canadian Division. The latter was preparing to enter the line that same night to take over from Ferry's 11th Division. Ferry's message was not well received by General Putz, the commander of the Belgian army detachment. He pointed out that "he didn't believe what the deserter had said because he had given such precise details of the organisation of the German front that it was clear that he had been sent to trick the Allies". In Putz's defence we can recognise that French intelligence was often inundated with wild declarations and fantastic rumours, but when provided with a number of clues it is preferable to consider them. And there were numerous clues, as on April 16th a Belgian intelligence report was distributed to the French.

"Use of suffocating gas. In Ghent, the Germans have urgently manufactured 20,000 tulle face masks that the soldiers will carry in a waterproof packet of 0.10 x 0.175 (agent). The facemasks, soaked in an appropriate liquid, will serve to protect the men against the suffocating gas that the Germans, notably the 26th Reserve Army Korps, intend to send towards the enemy lines. The men of this Korps are believed to have recently received special training, at Roulers, with regards to the handling of the gas cylinders; the gas cylinders are to be laid out on the ground with one battery of 20 cylinders every 40 metres (prisoner's statement)."

The British took Ferry's warning more seriously: they launched aerial reconnaissance patrols to try and pinpoint the cylinders but saw nothing unusual. None the less, all the troops of the 28th Division were put on maximum alert for the night of the 15th to 16th of April, during which time nothing happened. The day after, the relief of the 11th Division by the 1st Canadian Division got underway without incident, ending on the morning of April 17th.

The first German gas masks were very basic but this is easily explained by the fact that the attack was to take place a few minutes after the cloud had swept over the French lines; by that time it had already largely evaporated and the risks of suffocating were minimal. On April 16th 1915, the Belgians warn the French High Command that the Germans had made some mouth-protection devices in Ghent. (cf. text opposite) (IWM Q 51110)

A German 420 mm heavy howitzer, M model, also known as "Dicke Bertha". The Germans used artillery like this to fire on Ypres in April 1915. (Laparra collection, rights reserved)

A heavy bombardment begins

Another worrying sign appeared on April 17th 1915 when the Germans began a systematic heavy artillery bombardment of the town of Ypres. When the 11th Division left their 75 mm anti-aircraft batteries went with them and the Canadians did not replace them. The Germans immediately made the most of it by sending numerous artillery spotting aircraft over the outskirts of Ypres right up to Poperinge. On Monday 19th "Big Bertha", a 420 mm heavy howitzer, added its firepower to the bombardment, firing pairs of shells weighing up to more than 800 kg each. Lieutenant-Colonel Hankey, a British officer in commands of Ypres' square, noted in his War Diary: "The town was shelled from 10:00 a.m. till 12.30. Losses amongst the inhabitants: 9 killed, 8 wounded".

Another witness tells: "Now, Tuesday, even Ypres itself is bombarded. Enormous shells of a tonne, fired by the German 42 cm howitzer, have started to fall onto the old town. This "Big Bertha" fires at a rate of 10 shots per hour and causes horrific damage". The British were then forced to evacuate the last of the civilians still found in the old town. More than 2.000 persons were obliged to leave Ypres, some with the help of carts, others in trucks lent by the Canadian Division.

The effect of German shelling on Ypres in March and April 1915.
(IWM Q 61618)

The inhabitants of Ypres evacuate, April 18th 1915.
(IWM Q 61561)

It was subsequently forbidden for any civilian to return to Ypres.

The German order of battle on April 22nd

On April 20th, all the German units were in place. All they had to do was to wait for a favourable wind. At that time the 4th Army consisted of the following forces:

4th Army
Commander: General-Oberst Herzog Albrecht von Wurttemberg.

23rd Reserve Korps under General von Rathen,

45th Reserve Division,
89th Reserve Brigade: 201st and 202nd Reserve Infantry Regiments,
90th Reserve Brigade: 210th and 204th Reserve Infantry Regiments,
17th Reserve 'Jager' Batallion,

46th Reserve Division,
91st Reserve Brigade: 213th and 214th Reserve Infantry Regiments,
92nd Reserve Brigade: 215th and 216th Reserve Infantry Regiments,
18th Reserve 'Jager' Batallion,

26th Reserve Korps under General von Hugel,

52nd Reserve Division,
103rd Reserve Brigade: 237th and 238th Reserve Infantry Regiments,
104th Reserve Brigade: 239th and 240th Reserve Infantry Regiments,
24th Reserve 'Jager' Batallion,

51st Reserve Division,
101st Reserve Brigade: 233rd and 234th Reserve Infantry Regiments,
102nd Reserve Brigade: 235th and 236th Reserve Infantry Regiments,
23rd Reserve 'Jager' Batallion,

37th 'Landwehr' Brigade,
73rd and 74th 'Landwehr' Regiments,

2nd Reserve 'Ersatz' Brigade,
3rd and 4th Reserve 'Ersatz' Regiments,

27th Reserve Korps under General von Carlowitz,

38th 'Landwehr' Brigade,
77th and 78th 'Landwehr' Regiments,

53nd Reserve Division (Saxon),
105th Reserve Brigade: 241st and 242nd Reserve Infantry Regiments,
106th Reserve Brigade: 243rd and 244th Reserve Infantry Regiments,
25th 'Jager' Batallion,

54th Reserve Division (Wurttemburg),
107th Reserve Brigade: 245th and 246th Reserve Infantry Regiments,
108th Reserve Brigade: 247th and 248th Reserve Infantry Regiments,
28th Reserve 'Jager' Batallion,

15th Army Korps under General von Deimling,
39th Infantry Division,
61st Brigade: 126th and 132nd Infantry Regiments,
82nd Brigade: 171st and 172nd Infantry Regiments,

30th Infantry Division,
60th Brigade: 99th and 143rd Infantry Regiments,
85th Brigade: 105th and 186th Infantry Regiments,

German Artillery
(greater than 77 mm calibre)

23rd, 26th, 27th Reserve Korps:
Heavy Canons:
> 1 x 420 mm "Dicke Bertha"
> 20 x 210 mm
> 72 x 150 mm

Field guns:
> 4 x 125 mm
> 16 x 105 mm
> 34 canons, vintage or captured,

15th Army Korps:
Heavy Canons:
> 4 x 210 mm
> 12 x 150 mm

Field guns:
> 4 x 125 mm
> 2 x 105 mm
> 14 canons, vintage or captured,

The French order of battle

Two French divisions were committed to the front line and it would be they who experienced the first effects of the deadly gas.

French colonial troops in 1915. This picture, published in Germany, carried a caption saying it was Algerians using a mortar against German trenches. If they really were Zouaves it is hard to believe that the strange cylinder they are using is a mortar, even home-made. We do not know what it could be.
(Ysec collection)

Belgian Army Detachment

87th Territorial Division under General Roy,

173rd Brigade: 73rd and 74th Territorial Infantry Regiments,
174th Brigade: 76th, 79th, 80th Territorial Infantry Regiments,
186th Brigade: 100th and 102nd Territorial Infantry Regiments,

Front Line.

173rd Brigade: 9 companies from 74th Territorial Infantry Regiment and 9 companies from 73rd Territorial Infantry Regiment,

Second Line.

One and a half battalions of Territorial Infantrymen,
In reserve.
186th Brigade: 100th and 102nd Territorial Infantry Regiments,

45th (Algerian) Division under General Quiquandon,

90th Brigade: 2nd sub-division Zouaves (3 batallions), 1st Rifles (3 batallions), 1st and 3rd Africa battalions,;
91st Brigade: 7th Zouaves (3 batallions), 3rd sub-division Zouaves (3 batallions), 2 African battalions,

Front Line.

3 battalions of the 90th Brigade, 1st and 2nd Rifle battalions, 1st African battalion,

Second Line (2 km from the front, consisting of a series of strong points covering Pilckem and Het Sas),

1st battalion of 2nd Zouave sub-Division (90th Brigade) split between the centre of the line and the Pilckem – Langemarck road.
The "Cail" battalion, 7th Zouaves (91st Brigade) were placed behind the 1st battalion 2nd Zouaves, south of Pilckem,
Third Line.
A battalion of the 7th Zouaves guarded the bridges between Boesinghe and Ypres on the west bank of the Yser canal.

Elverdinghe Reserve Group.

Three battalions in reserve:
One battalion of infantry to the south of the Boesinghe – Elverdinghe road,
One battalion at Elverdinghe,
One African battalion between Elverdinghe and Woesten.

Artillery

Front Line,

As part of the 45th Algerian Division:
1 x 75 mm battery south of Zuydschoote,
2 x 90 mm batteries, 2 x 75 mm batteries, 1 x 95 mm batteries east of Boesinghe,
4 x 90 mm batteries, 2 x 75 mm batteries, east of Pilckem,

Rear,

1 x 120 mm battery and 1 x 95 mm battery covering the 87th Territorial Division,
1 x 120 mm battery covering the 45th Division,
1 x 75 mm battery (half at Boesinghe, half at Elverdinghe),

French troops in Belgium, October 1914. (IWM Q 57214)

A group of French interpreters attached to the British army, Flanders 1915. (IWM Q 60678)

Camaraderie between French and British soldiers after a football match, Ypres, February 1915.
(IWM Q 61557)
A British machine gun group, March 1915.
(IWM Q 61571)

The British order of battle

The British were not a part of the first gas attack and only the Canadian Division was subjected to the initial phase of the German offensive, on April 22nd. However, by the following day the British were totally engaged in the battle.

5th Army Corps *Commander Lieutenant-General Sir Herbert Plumer,*

(The front held by 5th Corps in the Ypres salient measured approximately 18 km. It started one km south of the village of Poelcappelle and finished a few hundred meters north of Hill 60.)

1st Canadian Division under Lieutenant-General E.A.H. Alderson.

First Line

3rd Canadian Infantry Brigade: 13th Battalion (Royal Highlanders of Canada) & 15th Battalion (48th Highlanders of Canada);

2nd Canadian Infantry Brigade: 8th Battalion (Winnepeg Rifles) & 5th Battalion (Western Cavalry).

Second and third positions

Four battalions of 2nd and 3rd Canadian Infantry Brigades:

One divisional reserve battalion situated between Saint-Jean et Ypres, 10th Battalion of the 2nd Brigade;

One battalion on the west bank of the Yser canal next to a temporary bridge at Brielen: 16th Battalion (Canadian Scottish);

A batallion of the 2nd and 3rd Canadian Infantry Brigades as brigade reserves: 14th Battalion (Royal Montreal Regiment) of the 3rd Brigade and 7th Battalion (British Columbia Regiment).

28th Division under Major-General E S Bulfin.

First Line

85th Brigade under Brigadier-General A J Chapman: 3rd Battalion Royal Fusiliers; 2nd Battalion East Surrey Regiment.

84th Brigade under Brigadier-General L J Bols: 1st Battalion The Welsh Regiment; 12th Battalion The London Regiment (Rangers); 1st Battalion The Suffolk Regiment.

83rd Brigade under Brigadier-General R C Boyle: 2nd Battalion The King's Own; 3rd Battalion The Monmouthshire Regiment; 1st Battalion The King's Own Yorkshire Light Infantry.

Second and third positions.

Two brigade reserve battalions near to Verlorenhoek: 2nd Battalion the Cheshire Regiment & 1st Battalion the Monmouthshire Regiment;

Three battalions near to Saint-Jean, north-east of Ypres: 2nd Battalion the Buffs, 3rd Battalion Middlesex Regiment_;

Two and a half battalions to the west Ypres.

27th Division under Major-General T D'O Snow.

First Line

Three battalions of each of the following Brigades were in the front line:
80th Brigade under Brigadier-General W E B Smith,
81st Brigade under Brigadier-General H L Croker,
82nd Brigade under Brigadier-General J R Longley,

Second and third positions

Two battalions in the Sanctuary Wood sector near to Hooge.

Two battalions were to the north west of Ypres and one near to Vlamertinghe as Divisional reserves.

Reserves

1st Canadian Infantry Brigade under Brigadier-General M S Mercer,

13th Brigade (of 2nd Corps) in the Vlamertinghe sector

Sir Herbert Plumer

The Belgian army.

The Belgian army is often forgotten in the history of the first gas attack. It is true that it was the French units that were attacked but the 6th Belgian Division, which was to the north of the 87th Territorial Division's lines, was, of course, directly concerned by the battle.

Commander Willy Breton described his men thus: "dressed like tramps, badly equipped, driven mad by the rain, frozen to the bone, shivering in the icy fog, up to their knees in the mire, the men laboured without rest under continuous enemy fire, rarely taking breaks, and only laying down their entrenching tools to stand guard, rifle in hand, in their mud-filled trenches."

6th Belgian Army Division

18th Mixed Brigade.
    1st Grenadier Regiment,
    2nd Grenadier regiment,
    18th Company of machine guns,
    Artillery Group,
    Gendarme Platoon,
19th Mixed Brigade.
    1st Rifle Regiment,
    3rd Rifle Regiment,
    19th Company of machine guns,
    Artillery Group,
    Gendarme Platoon,
20th Mixed Brigade.
    2nd Rifle Regiment,
    20th Company of machine guns,
    Artillery Group,
    Gendarme Platoon,
Divisional Troops.
    1st Cavalry Regiment,
    6th Artillery regiment,
    6th Battalion, Divisional Engineers,
    Transport Corps,
    6th Section, Field Telegraphists,

The 1st Divisions artillery was brought up in support, as well as the Army's heavy artillery, ie: a 150 Schnieder battery supplied with only 700 shells for 12 guns.

Belgian machine gunners and their dogs leave the station to head for the front line. (IWM Q 48445)

Two Belgian infantry snipers in a haystack. (collection Ysec)

A DEADLY CLOUD
ENVELOPES
THE FRENCH LINES

(Pages 38-39) A German gas attack. Without a doubt this scene takes place in a training area as the trenches are remarkably intact. This picture was not taken in Flanders; no photographs exist of the first gas attack showing the green-yellow chlorine cloud. The event is believed to have taken place to the north of Beauséjour, that is to say on the Champagne front (or behind it), at an unknown date. (IWM Q 23755)

(Above). The German trenches emit waves of gas. This view, even better than the previous, gives an idea of the attack of April 22nd 1915. (Ysec collection)

The morning of April 22nd 1915 was glorious. The French worked hard to improve their trenches, which were still in a pitiful state, and the Canadians did the same. 20 kilometres or so behind the Steenstraat front, Claude Prieur, the naval infantryman previously mentioned, wrote in his diary: "Thursday April 22nd. The pleasures of spring at camp. The sun invites us to go out; the tennis courts on the beach are crowded. The marine officers congregate there with their comrades, the Zouaves, and even the Territorials (…) By chance I came across M. Robert d'Humières, of whom I had read with such pleasure his beautiful translations of Kipling. He had joined up as a Lieutenant with the Zouaves. We did not think alas, either of us, chatting together, that two or three days later, the gas attack would be fatal for him".

The beautiful day is only disturbed in the afternoon, on the northern Ypres front, by the violent anti-aircraft barrage that was thrown up against a French observation aircraft. The Germans wanted at all costs to prevent their preparations from being discovered. Around 5.20 pm, Colonel Mordacq receives a telephone call from Commandant Villeveix of

the 1st Machine Guns. He relates thus the events: "Gasping for breath, voice broken, hardly understandable, he told me "that he was being savagely attacked, huge columns of yellow smoke coming from the German trenches were, at that moment, sweeping across his whole front line; that the infantry were starting to evacuate the trenches and fall back; many fell suffocated". I admit that, when hearing such words, and, especially with such a voice, I asked myself for a moment if the Commandant had not lost his mind or was suffering from one of these cerebral strokes which I had frequently seen at the beginning of the campaign in the war of mobility, especially during the battles of the Chipotte (September 1914). A gas attack was the last thing I would have thought of, never having considered the possibility and neither having ever heard talk of it since my arrival in Belgium".

But soon, Mordacq heard volleys of shots and a violent bombardment. Not long after, Commandant Fabry also called him on the telephone with news as worrying as that of Villevaleix'. He declared "that he was going to be obliged to leave his Command Post as he was unable to breath; that,

Some French liaison officers near Messines, south of Ypres, at the end of 1914. It is often forgotten but the presence of the French army around Ypres saved the town during the winter 1914-1915, after the near annihilation of the British Expeditionary Force during the first battle of Ypres. (IWM Q 60666)

41

around him, whole groups of infantry were falling suffocated or killed when trying to break through the artillery barrage that the Germans were raining down on the reserve positions; the situation was no longer tenable, we were trapped between the gas and the bombardment".

Jumping onto his horse, Mordacq rushed towards the trenches. He relates "three of four hundred meters away from Boesinghe, we were seized with a violent prickling in the nose and throat; our ears started to buzz, breathing became difficult, an unbearable smell of chlorine reigned around us. We soon had to dismount, the horses, uncomfortable, frightened, refusing to gallop or trot. So we gained Boesinghe on foot, then went on to the bridges. At the outskirts of the village the scene was more than appalling, it was tragic. Soldiers were fleeing in all directions: territorials, regulars, infantry, Zouaves, gunners, (tunics torn off or completely undone, cravats askew), running all over the place like madmen, begging for water in loud screams, spitting blood, some even rolling on the ground desperately fighting for breath.

The testimony of a frontline doctor

A doctor of the 1st Africa battalion was at Pilkem during the German attack. He heard the shooting and placed himself behind a small wall to observe the trenches with Adjutant

A Flemish farm on fire after German shelling, March 1915. (IWM Q 61604)

Cordier: "We then saw, on all sides, the men leaving the trenches and retreating towards the village, without understanding, at that time, the reason for the panic. A few seconds later, turning to our left, we saw that the sky was completely obscured by a yellow-green cloud that looked like an approaching storm. Next thing we knew the suffocating gas enveloped us. I had the impression that I was looking through glasses with green lenses. At the same time I felt the effect of the gas in my chest: throat burning, chest pains, breathlessness and spitting blood, vertigo. We all thought we were doomed; poor Cordier was pitiful to look at, he had turned purple and was incapable of walking".

Other view of the French Field Hospital set up in the church of Dickebus in November 1914. At that time the term 'ambulance' does not refer to a vehicle like nowadays, but an entire aid facility. This one was more than likely set up in the church and the vehicles of the military health service provide for the arrival and evacuation of the wounded. (IWM Q 57331)

Octave Béliard was another doctor who related the effects of the gas attack from his position on the second line: "We watched in astonishment as, from out of the hail of bullets, a leaderless horde came rushing up towards us, fleeing. Entire regiments had thrown down their weapons, turned their backs on the enemy (…) People cried: "Save yourselves! We are lost!" Men were rolling on the ground, convulsing, coughing, vomiting, spitting blood. And a terrible smell, swept along by the wind, entered our nostrils. The panic was total; the injured were dragged away, others threw themselves to the ground and groaned, those desperate to flee clambered over the bodies… Slowly, as the effect of surprise subsided, troops rallied and returned to their combat positions… But it

Another Flemish farm burnt down following German shelling, March 1915. Bombardments increased in April before the gas attack. (IWM Q 61552)

was a nerve-wrecking time, one of those times when you lose faith. I had soaked my handkerchief in water and held it in front of my mouth and nose. I climbed onto the talus, as much to find some air as by curiosity. From one end of the horizon to the other, the sky was opaque, a strange and sinister green. In this deathly pale night, houses burnt like oily torches".

A Belgian soldier's testimony

A Belgian grenadier, quoted by Commander Willy Breton, gave the following eye witness account: "Between the Belgian and the French front lines was a space of about 200 meters where a dozen houses of the Steenstraat hamlet stood, including a small brasserie where we had installed a listening post. There we were, eight men and a corporal (…)

It was a dazzling spring day; a light northern wind blew. All was so calm that we hardly even thought about the war

when, suddenly, around 6.30 in the afternoon [18 h 30, Belgian time, one hour ahead of French time] we saw thick smoke rise up out of the German trenches opposite us. Surprise and curiosity glued us to the spot. None of us could have guessed, at that moment, what it was. As the smoke cloud thickened we thought that the dug-outs in the German trenches had caught fire. The cloud slowly came towards us but, under the effect of the wind, we saw it drift to the right over the French lines. Only the outer edges of the vapour cloud reached us; it was not as thick but released such a singular smell, and seized me at

A position of the Royal West Kent Regiment near Ypres, April 1915. The ground has already been churned up by shellfire in the sector. It is without a doubt the western most part of the salient. It was in the Hill 60 sector that the most violent combat took place prior to the German gas attack. (IWM Q 61568)

the throat so that I thought for a moment that I was going to suffocate. Suddenly, everyone cried: "An attack, the Boches are here…" I looked to where the cries were coming from, it was the French soldiers that occupied positions around Steenstraat bridge and were running towards our trenches. Many fell on the way. When our Corporal called out to find out what was happening, I heard them answer "We've been gassed".

The British become involved in the drama

The British, to the right of the French lines, suddenly head violent fire from French field artillery which they found surprising as the Germans only fired on distant targets using heavy pieces. Many officers thought that the artillery of the 45th Division was carrying out ranging shots. But other officers, situated on the heights, saw two curious yellow-green clouds moving from one end of Langemarck to the other. Among the British witnesses was General Smith-Dorrien, commander of the 2nd Army, and General Snow, who commanded the 27th Division, and, of course General Anderson, commanding officer of the 1st Canadian Division.

A British soldier, who was in reserve to the north-east of Ypres at the time, described in detail what he saw on April

22nd for The Times not long after the battle. "On Thursday 22nd April around 5.30 in the afternoon, one of our patrols signalled that our French allies, to the left of the Canadian division, suddenly fell back along the road from Ypres to Langemarck (…) A living wall of green fog, about 1.20m high, moved towards the French lines over a width of about 180 meters. The wall of smoke grew higher and higher until soon the whole sector had disappeared. Suddenly, French rifle fire grew in intensity, but it gradually subsided, as is often the case when soldiers don't fire on a particular target but simply try to defend themselves by firing in the hope of hitting somebody. Soon we heard strange cries coming from the green cloud. The cries became weaker and incoherent. Then, masses of soldiers staggered from the cloud and collapsed. Many did not appear hurt but their faces were marked with expressions of terror. These retreating wrecks were part of the best soldiers in the world; their discipline and their courage were almost legendary. At that moment they were reeling like drunkards".

A British position near Blauepoort Farm, on the outskirts of Ypres. The wood is on a slight rise that allows the building of underground shelters. Note, none the less, that the appearance of the place is not that much tidier than the French trenches. (IWM Q 61566)

Some German accounts

The German history of the Great War, entitled Der Völkerkrieg (tome V), quotes many German witnesses. One of these accounts was signed by an infantryman, probably belonging to the 52nd Reserve Division. His testimony must be taken with caution, as he seems to embellish what he sees and what he does: "We jump out of the trenches and in a few minutes, we reach the enemy trench, crushing all attempts at resistance from the enemy. We continue, three trench lines are captured. We are now in the main positions where we find the artillery! Who would have thought that we would capture canons today? Nine in all, including brand new guns. We thought that the enemy opposition to our attack would be very different and are very happy to have suffered only light casualties. Our artillery had done its job well in "softening up" the French and the British.

The sight that greeted us in the captured positions was quite grotesque. Our heavy shells had opened up enormous crevasses in the earth. The shelters have been destroyed. Amongst the debris are shredded corpses and dismembered limbs. Not only are there white bodies lying on the ground

The site of the first gas attack as represented on an orientation table. (Ysec)

but also black, brown, yellow and red! There is a complete mixture of races; death has taken a terrible harvest (…) There is also, amongst the prisoners that we take, a large number of coloured troops who are visibly happy to have been captured by the Germans and to have had their lives spared. We were stunned, as we thought that there were only British soldiers opposite us. Now we see that we fight against people of many different races. We were victorious and the moment we had been waiting for, when we could claim the enemy's trenches, had finally come. They could come back, we were waiting for them!"

We can pick out of this account some errors and omissions. The main error was to talk about British troops when the attack was directed against the two French Divisions north of Ypres. Could it be that the German infantrymen were not informed of the nationality of the troops opposing them? That seems doubtful. As for the racial mix of the Allied troops, it was exaggerated. There were obviously no "red-skins" in the 45th Colonial Division, nor were there any Asian soldiers. The biggest error, however, is the total

The grave of Bekhti Beloued, gassed on April 22nd. (Ysec collection)

49

Due to the large number of Breton soldiers killed during the first gas attack, many monuments built in the Breton tradition have been erected around Ypres. This memorial cross, set up after the Second World War, is obviously inspired from Breton crosses. It is situated in the French national cemetery in Saint-Charles de Potijze, west of Ypres, where the French dead from 1914 and 1915 are buried. (Ysec collection)

lack of any reference to the gas and its effects. By contrast, the effects of the heavy artillery are exaggerated. We see elsewhere that the Germans make little reference to the use of suffocating gas.

Another soldier recalls: "We have finally achieved our objective. We have crossed the Yser canal and are dug-in on the other side (…) Dozens of barges are ready and waiting to take us across the canal which is already full of soldiers swimming across, holding their weapons above their heads". This account suggests that the German engineers had followed or even accompanied the first waves of the attack. A boat bridge was quickly put in place. But of course the barges could not have been brought up by the Germans. They simply happened to be on the canal when the offensive took place.

A third German account is, without doubt, the most interesting. Our witness belongs to the reserve troops or, in any case, was not part of the first wave of attacks. He writes: "We reach our own frontline trenches which have been boarded over so that we could cross easily. After having covered the 150 meters of no man's land with some difficulty we enter the enemy's frontline trenches. It's there that we find the first casualties. It is evening and we can see the gently swinging lamps of the medical team looking after the wounded. Then we meet the first group of French prisoners. We are surprised to see that they are not the proud sons of La Grande Nation which we were expecting; they are old men with grimy faces. Among them are also black soldiers with colourful uniforms. We also see civilians in this column, on horse carts, especially women and children. Scruffy dogs rub themselves against the wheels of the carts and the legs of people on foot (…) Columns of artillery and munitions overtake us. Regimental Staff Officers pass through, galloping on their horses. As we move forward into what remains of the enemy's positions we discover more and more sad cases. A growing number of military prisoners and scared civilians pass on the road. A herd of terrified cows is driven towards the rear. All walk in the direction from whence we came. As

Two dead from December 1914 : territorials of the 73rd Territorial Infantry Regiment. (Ysec collection)

The grave of Mohamed Ben El Hamdi, a soldier of the 9th Native Infantry Regiment. (Ysec collection)

we advance our heavy artillery fire shell after shell over our heads in the direction of Ypres".

The presence of old men is easily explained, as the German soldier in question has undoubtedly passed through the sector held by the 87th Territorial Division. As for the rest, the most surprising in this description is the presence of civilians. They are never mentioned in the reports or descriptions of the battle of Ypres but their presence is nonetheless understandable, as the German advance during the first hours of the offensive was both deep and fast. In little more than half an hour the German troops covered three to four kilometres and capture Pilckem, their first objective.

What became of the artillery ?

One of the blunders of the French High Command was to have left a large number of field artillery pieces just behind the front line. Colonel Mordacq, on the scene as soon as he heard about the new attack on the banks of the canal, recalls what happened: "I was also able to interrogate a few artillery officers who escaped the horror and who valiantly laid down a barrage of artillery fire from their positions next to the bridges, using the few artillerymen that they had succeeded

The beautiful Breton cross erected in the old sector of the 87th Territorial Division, between Pilckem and Boesinghe. (Ysec collection)

The monument to the victims of the first gas attack, in Steenstraat. The first monument was destroyed by the Germans during the Second World War. On the base of the mound on which the great cross is erected we find the order of battle of the French and Belgian units present during the second battle of Ypres. (Ysec collection)

The grave of Emile Maurer, a soldier of the 1st Zouaves, killed on April 23rd 1915 and buried in the cemetery of Potijze. (Ysec collection)

in pulling together. Mad with anger, spitting blood, eyes bulging, they told me that all their guns had fallen into the hands of the Germans, and I can still see them now, begging me to organise an immediate counter-attack to recapture them. But with whom, and with what? I tried to make them understand that, to prepare such an attack, we needed infantry: where were they? And especially artillery, to prepare and support the advance; we didn't even have one piece.

They gave me more details: barely a few minutes after the beginning of the attack and the gas cloud they suddenly saw the Germans appear a few hundred meters from their guns.

Despite the gas the supporting troops opened fire straight away, sending forth a hail of machine gun fire until they ran out of ammunition: then it was all over. Luckily the gas cloud had passed a little to the north of the batteries. The Germans, their faces covered with a sort of mask, had suffered heavy losses and had stopped for a moment. Shortly after we distinctly heard the shouts of their officers, "Vorwaerts! Vorwaerts!" and the rolling artillery barrage that preceded them increased in intensity. Finally, enemy units appeared to the right and to the left. We immediately spiked the guns, abandoning them (we lost 3 x 75 mm and 2 x 120 mm guns); a large number of support troops could not get away and were taken prisoner.

The Breton monument shows the garrison towns of the territorial regiments: Vitré, Guingamp and Saint-Brieuc (Ysec collection)

The nightmare of the Territorials

Accounts relating to the 87th Territorial Division, composed of Bretons and Normans, are rare. Even General Mordacq, in his book Le Drame de l'Yser (the Drama of the Yser), more often quotes the Belgian grenadiers than the

The Het-Sas lock today and, below, a lock photographed during the battle, to the west of the Ypres salient. (collection Ysec and IWM Q 61630)

Territorials. And yet it is clearly the latter who suffered the gas attack. The 173rd brigade is literally wiped out by the yellow-green chlorine cloud. Doctor Nel, already mentioned, notes quite simply: "the chlorine cloud passed over Triangular Wood and Pilckem, tainted with white, yellow, green; the atmosphere is filled with an acrid taste, irritating,

that makes breathing painful; the shooting rattles on and the bullets fall in Boesinghe".

Unfortunately, to describe the fall-back of the French troops, he then borrows from John Buchan. Whatever the talents of the famous English author and novelist he was not present on the spot and so his testimony has no documentary value despite, or rather because of, his search for sensationalism. And so he writes: "… they had fallen in front of [a diabolical machine] much more than in front of human terror. Behind them lay hundreds of their dead comrades, lips twisted in a terrifying grimace, faces horribly blue". Nel did not see what became of the front line troops. He contented himself in writing that "a few days later only a couple of hundred men could be accounted for, survivors of the 173rd brigade, and a lot of them owed their lives to the fact that, for one reason or another (ill, cooks, office workers, etc) they were not in the front line at that time".

Later, he points out: "coming along the railway track from Langemarck, the 45th[s] sector, were many groups containing young soldiers, Zouaves and regulars, hurrying towards Boesinghe, but many fall, out of breath, suffocating". The reserve units of the Territorial Division stand to. It is notably the case of the 79th Territorial Infantry Regiment, of which the battles of the 2nd battalion are described in detail by

Another view of the Het-Sas lock today, on the Yser canal. The area is once again peaceful and it is difficult to imagine that this place was host to one of the worst episodes of the First World War.
(Ysec collection)

The Yser canal is quite wide and constituted a natural barricade that the French would exploit. (Ysec collection)

Doctor Nel: "The Yser, where the Flanders offensive broke down last November, shows herself once more to be our ally in this second battle of Ypres. The waters themselves come to our aid and the heavy chlorine clouds die there at the end of their race, absorbed as they cross the waters (…) Forever methodical, and knowing the importance of the road and rail bridges, the Germans had quickly sent forward groups of soldiers on bicycles to capture these strategically important points. But seeing that they were defended, and understanding the impossibility of the advanced guard to reach them, they immediately set up machine guns and shooting positions in the neighbouring houses controlling these crossings".

8th Company carry out a reconnaissance patrol in the sector of l'Huilerie to at least try and maintain a presence. But it was too late: "soon, on all sides, slipping along the hedges, the Germans arrived at the canal and our reconnaissance patrol, realising that the enemy infiltration was widespread, and that it exposed itself to capture, considered that its mission was finished and came back to take up their places in the trenches, as part of the main battalion, in preparation for the defence of the canal". In the mean time, survivors and stragglers continued to rush for the Boesinghe bridges: "Some

We often think that, apart from the French and, to a certain extent, the Belgians, only the Canadians were involved in the second battle of Ypres. This is an error as shown by these graves of Scottish soldiers from the Seaforth Highlanders, buried where they fell on April 25th 1915, in the cemetery of Cheddar Valley, near what was 'le bois des cuisiniers' or Kitchener's Wood for the British. (Ysec collection)

regulars, some Zouaves and some territorials of the 73rd and 74th fleeing, half suffocated, continued to arrive at the road bridge; we hurry to let them through and they take up positions next to our troops in the trenches. It is there, dishevelled, that we find today what is left of the proud regiments of the 45th division that, just a few days before, had marched with such pomp through Boesinghe when advancing to occupy the Langemarck sector. Surprised by the gas, many of them had started to follow the railway tracks to escape from the enemy and return to our lines. Many fell on the way, suffocated; the others managed to get to Boesinghe and came to give us a hand by standing with us in the defence of the bridges".

The race between the Germans and the 1st battalion of the 79th Territorial Infantry Regiment (TIR)

Doctor Nel summarises quite well the situation which the 1st battalion of the 79th TIR must have faced: "From its point of view the 1st battalion received the same orders and accomplished the same mission as the 2nd, which took it north along the trenches next to the canal up to the lock at Het-Sas. But there its role became more complicated. In fact, at this point, close to the edge of Triangular Wood, the gas had permitted the Germans to reach the canal quickly and so, when the companies of the 1st battalion of the 79th TIR arrived, the lock was already in the hands of the enemy. After having dug in they had set up positions on the western bank of the canal and threatened to take Boesinghe from the rear".

The Canadian monument at St-Julien, situated in the middle of the 1st Canadian Infantry Division lines on April 22nd 1915. The plaque visible at the bottom of the monument is reproduced opposite. (Ysec collection)

THIS·COLUMN·MARKS·THE
BATTLEFIELD·WHERE·18,000
CANADIANS·ON·THE·BRITISH
LEFT·WITHSTOOD·THE·FIRST
GERMAN·GAS·ATTACKS·THE
22-24·APRIL·1915·2,000·FELL
AND·LIE·BURIED·NEARBY

Their mission consisted, on the one hand, to hold the canal trenches and, on the other, to contain the German bridgehead on the west of the Het-Sas lock. It was, of course, the second mission that was the more difficult, but the Territorials acquitted themselves well: "Under the enthusiastic orders of Commandant Cordier, whilst the company laid down heavy fire over the entire line, some sections quickly scraped shallow trenches facing north-east, covering the flank of the enemy arriving at Het-Sas. A well placed machine gun, handled with considerable sang-froid by Adjutant Lefrène who, his loader lying injured at his feet, continued to fire non-stop on his own, providing tremendous support. Soon these right angled trenches, providing a protective screen to the canal which was threatened with being overrun, set up a counterattack which halts the Germans at the lock and pushes them back towards Steenstraat".

The terrain played in favour of the French as the Ysel canal formed an impassable barrier. What is more, "along its banks, trenches, dug many weeks ago and dried out by the fine weather, offered our troops both a refuge and a first rate fighting position". Opposite our waiting troops, who were well prepared and well protected, the enemy poured out into

This view, shot from a trench on the edge of the canal, was taken in the British sector and not next to Het-Sas and Boesinghe. Even so, it shows quite remarkably how a single battalion of the 79th TIR could have prevented the Germans from crossing the canal. (IWM Q 61579)

*The Breton cross at
Saint-Charles of Potijze.
(Ysec collection)*

the open across the sloping ground that led down towards the opposite bank. Immediately heavy firing crackled from our trenches and began causing heavy losses to the enemy. We could not have found ourselves in a more favourable position: our troops, so well dug in behind the canal that they were almost impregnable, stood firm; firing at will they caused enormous losses to the enemy who advanced in compact groups with no protective cover". Thus, after the initial surprise, the Breton and Normandy Territorials managed to constitute a defensive front solid enough to hold the Germans while awaiting re-enforcements. The situation was more confused and more dangerous to the south as the 45th division had disappeared, leaving a worrying breach in the front that the Canadians, even by trying to extend their left flank towards the west, were incapable of covering by themselves.

Foch summarises the situation to Joffre

On April 23rd Foch sent a quite succinct report to Joffre showing that, many hours after the beginning of the German offensive, the High Command still did not have a very clear idea of the situation on the ground. Nonetheless, it addressed the basics: "Mon Général, last night we had a nasty surprise. The Germans sent over large quantities of a suffocating gas, penetrating to a depth of more than one kilometre along the whole front through Steenstraat, Langemarck and further to the east. At 5.00pm all our front line territorials at Triangular Wood and in the surrounding area were completely suffocated and fell back in disarray to Boesinghe; they suffered less on the 2nd line, nonetheless they abandoned the Boesinghe bridgehead and the artillery that was there. We do not yet know how many guns may have been saved. At the same time our rifle regiment of the 45th division, based at Langemarck and the surrounding areas, lost that territory with heavy casualties and retreated to the S.E. of Boesinghe (left bank of Yser). It was all over by 5.30pm. At the same time the English left

The Canadian monument at Kitchener's Wood, erected not long ago on the battle field. The wood itself no longer exists and the whole sector may soon be disfigured by a motorway. On the base of the monument is found a map and a short historical text in Flemish and in English: "During the night of April 22nd 1915, after the first chemical attack in history, the 1 "Canadians" Battalion and the 16th Battalion "The Canadian Scottish" Battalion recaptured Kitchener's Wood". (Ysec collection)

B / 13308-13315

ERNST RICHTER MELDEREITER • 10.5.1915
HERMANN HÄNEL ERSATZ-RESERVIST • 8.5.1915
PAUL STÖRL SOLDAT • 31.10.1914
PAUL HÖSE SOLDAT • 18.2.1916
ANTON HEIMHILGER ERSATZ-RESERVIST • 31.10.1914
SEBASTIAN ZIEGLER UNTEROFFIZIER • 31.10.1914
ADOLF ORTWEIN WEHRMANN • 27.10.1914
THEODOR BURKHARDT FREIWILLIGER • 24.10.1914

WILHELM STROTHMANN SERGEANT • 13.5.1915
GEORG KANITZKI SOLDAT • 30.7.1915
STEFAN WAGNER ERSATZ-RESERVIST • 1.11.1914
KARL BERTSCH WEHRMANN • 31.10.1914
JAKOB WILD INFANTERIST • 3.10.1914
GEORG PFALLER UNTEROFFIZIER • 25.10.1914
PAUL BEUTEL UNTEROFFIZIER • 26.10.1914
ERNST BURGHARDT ERSATZ-RESERVIST • 25.10.1914

B / 13131-13124

The Germans also suffered losses, especially when arriving at the banks of the Yser canal and, most of all, during the engagements that followed the period of surprise following the first gas attack. On this stone, in the German cemetery of Langemarck, are found the names of soldiers who fell during the battles of October 1914, but also those of the month of May 1915. The battle had, in fact, continued at Ypres until mid May without either party gaining the upper hand. (Ysec collection)

flank fell back on Saint-Julien and reformed along the old front at Strombeke (1,600 meters west of Wallemolen). Our line was breached along a length of 3.5 kilometres between our right flank and the English left; the road to Ypres is clear. At the same time the Germans took Steenstraat and Het-Sas but they were soon retaken".

In the first instance we note that the battle does not take place on the Yser, but on the Yser canal at Ypres. As for the rest, Foch puts great emphasis on the speed of the action as he considers it as completed by 5.30pm, half an hour after the beginning of the attack. He talks here of the first phase, the quick German advance, as the battle does not really come to a halt. What Foch does not say, but what he must surely know, is that with the opening of a breach of 3.5 kilometres in the French lines the road to Ypres is open. The Allied High Command was forced to fill this gaping hole in its lines as early as that evening by launching a counter-attack with the meagre elements at its disposition, that is to say its few reserves bolstered by a few stragglers, with no artillery support and no coordination with those Canadian units that were not affected by the first phase of the battle.

A foxhole near Blauepoort Farm, in April 1915. The steel helmet had not yet appeared in any army, no more so than in the British than in the German or the French. (IWM Q 61567)

THE ALLIED COUNTER-ATTACK OF APRIL 22ND - 23RD 1915

The following pictures were
taken near Hazebrouck,
in March 1915, only a few
weeks before the German
gas attack. They show a
column of Parisian buses
requisitioned for the trans-
portation of the troops. The
faces of the infantrymen that
we can make out behind the
windows of the buses are not
young. They are more than
likely from the 87th Breton
and Normand Territorial
Division. These same buses
will enable the French
High Command to quickly
bring up reinforcements in
the threatened sectors of
Boesinghe, Het-Sas, Lizerne.
(IWM Q 61564
and Q 61563)

och, in the message he sent to Joffre, summarised the
measures taken to immediately try to stop the German
advance before it was too late. As always, Foch proved
to be over optimistic. He writes: "Fortunately, as early as
5.00 this morning the Zouaves, positioned between the Yser
and the Ypres-Pilkem road, three English battalions coming
from Ypres and the Canadian Division all linked-up on the
right bank of the Yser and returned to the battle, whilst we
maintained our defensive positions opposite Steenstraat, at
the retaken Het-Sas, at Boesinghe and along the Yser. This
well coordinated offensive has advanced strongly throughout
the afternoon.

At this moment we are also attacking Steenstraat. I do
not yet know of the results. I have brought up two battalions
of Zouaves from Nieuport and a group of 75, already committed; the 10th Army's 153rd Division, with two artillery
groups, is currently being disembarked. The English left was
reinforced with seven battalions; this evening it has a further
infantry division and three cavalry divisions; on our left the
Belgian Army is supporting our attack on Steenstraat and the
right bank of the Yser with many howitzer or cannon batteries. So we have, at present, all the means necessary to launch
tomorrow, the 24th, a vigorous offensive with the objective

A rare and remarkable image of three
French infantrymen in the Grand Square
of Ypres, December 1914. The Cloth Hall
has already lost its roof.
(IWM Q 51222)

Teams of horses (French) in a Flemish village during the winter 1914-1915. The fact that the sign of the inn is written in French does not necessarily mean that the picture was taken in France rather than in Belgium. (IWM Q 57269)

of recapturing lost ground. I hold a brigade and two groups of the 10th Army ready to be mobilised if need be. A perfect co-ordination and understanding continues to exist amongst the Allied forces".

In fact, the Allied counter-attack started well before 05.00 in the morning on April 23rd. As early as the evening of the 22nd some attacks failed without it being possible to know where the orders for the counter-attack came from. In his book Mordacq is not very coherent with his explanations. After visiting the battlefield at Boesinghe, where he gave the order to blow up the bridges on the Yser canal (an excellent decision), he returned to his command post in the castle of Elverdinghe. He noted: "I stayed on the telephone for more than half an hour, however I could not obtain any precise details for the simple reason that, from the top to the bottom of the chain of command, nobody knew what was going on. Everywhere everyone felt the same agony, the same anxiety, the same anguish". Mordacq continues by indicating that, should the Germans continue their attack, the only way to stop them would be to counter-attack and "I have already given that order... but with no real hope of success, as the essential element to support the counter-attack was missing: the artillery; I did not have a single canon at my disposition."

Why give such an order with no hope of success? It is even more surprising that on page 119 of his book Mordacq writes with regards to the counter-attacks of the morning of April 23rd, decided by Foch: "As for the French counter-attack, planned for 4.30am, it was totally crazy that people should be making decisions without having the slightest idea as to what was happening on the ground. Besides, where are we going to find the troops to organise it? Similar events will reoccur many times during the days of April 22nd, 23rd and 24th 1915 and afterwards, just because some French divisional commanders did not come and find out what was going on themselves".

Strong sentiments, but then, why this counter-attack as soon as the 22nd without having the means? The answer, which does not come from Mordacq himself, is without doubt the following: believing that the Germans were going to continue their march on Ypres, Mordacq did not see any other solution to stop them other than to try a last ditch effort with his remaining troops, even if the chances of success

French liaison officers in a Flemish town, 1915. We do not know where the photograph was taken but the officers, as they are liaison officers, are obviously in the British or Belgian sector. (IWM Q 60676)

were thin. At 4.30am the situation is no longer the same, as the Germans have well and truly stopped.

The failure of the first counter-attack

If Mordacq is not very coherent in his position concerning the counter-attack, Doctor Nel, who is certainly not a career soldier, is unambiguous: "Alas, in short order, the understanding of what we were being commanded to do descends upon our lines like a veil of cruel and barbarian mourning: "Counter-attack"! that is to say, fix bayonets, climb out of the trenches and counter-attack. The order is transmitted without enthusiasm, blind and unquestioning. It is the knee-jerk reflex of defence, the fever-driven reaction of a High Command staggering before the surprise they did not foresee; the mechanical order of counter-attack spreads out from the area where the action was taking place, repeating itself over and over again".

Of course, in the situation which the 1st battalion (of the 79th TIR) found itself, a bayonet charge in front of a canal where the enemy is in control of the banks is a derisory absurdity, totally unrealistic, but all explanations, all accounting is useless. The order is renewed with military insistence, no questions asked, no discussion of the insanity of the situation allowed, we must carry out orders, obey straight away (...) "Over the top, fix bayonets and charge" The sacrificial bell sounds. The companies fix bayonets, the

officers and enlisted men in front climb up onto the bank. Of course the Germans, on the other bank, on whom the bullets rain down and who take fire without being able to fire back, could not have hoped for such a piece of luck and the result was felt not long after. The movement hardly had the time to deploy before, in less than a few minutes, a whole list of killed and injured bore witness to blind obedience. The enemy were able to select their victims, living targets offering themselves up to death: the officers, the enlisted men, recognisable by their uniforms, were the first to fall. All of the 1st company – under the command of lieutenant Bourdin - adjutant Guéraud, sergeant de Lancesseur, remarkable for their bravery and leadership, are mortally wounded. From the 3rd company lieutenant Casanova, who commanded the company, is killed, adjutant Dupont is injured. Captain Lion, of the 2nd, injured in the neck, is considered missing, etc. In short, three company commanders in four are put out of combat, the best we had (…). Could not certain orders be considered as murder? Can they not then be judged as crimes? All these dead, if they came back, would they not stand as

In the British lines, March 1915, Bluff sector. This British officer is 2nd lieutenant Barclay, commander of the Motor Machine Gun Unit, who will be killed at Hooge in August 1915. He is at the entrance to a dug out with a steaming mug of tea. Even if his rank is not visible, his riding boots and jodhpurs immediately identify him as an officer.
(IWM Q 61572)

This British corporal of the Royal West Kent Regiment photographed in the Bluff sector, shows off a rare and interesting weapon: a British hand grenade. The photograph was taken at the end of March 1915 and shows what all the eye witnesses confirm: that the weather was spring-like. (IWM Q 61577)

accusers? But military justice was nothing if not rudimentary, inflexible, dispensed as an example on poor devils sometimes more ignorant than guilty, if not even innocent, but they were only NCOs or soldiers". In the 45th Division's sector Colonel Mordacq's counter-attack was led by six companies of the 7th Zouaves Battalion. It did not advance very far, and tried to link up with the Canadians, but the breach remained important.

The British counter-attack

As early as 5.55pm the Canadian artillery received the order to support the 45th French Division. Five minutes later

eight batteries were able to support the French. At 6.30pm, the 3rd Canadian Brigade received the order to stand ready to counter-attack. An hour later the brigade informed its division that it could only provide one battalion (the 14th Canadian Battalion), which would not be very effective. But, none the less, at 8.52pm the 1st Canadian Division gives the order to launch this battalion in recapturing Kitchener's Wood. Finally, it is two other battalions, the 10th and the 16th, advancing from the rear, that would be thrown into Kitchener's Wood from 11.30pm, to clear the wood and, if possible, re-establish contact with the French. The counter-attack does not actually start until after midnight, on April 23rd. The wood is finally retaken but this does not allow the restoration of a continuous front with the French. Mordacq summarises thus the end of the Canadian operation: "The two battalions recapture the wood but, in turn, are attacked by heavy forces and were nearly annihilated without being able to get in contact with the 7th Zouaves".

*A few of the Ypres market halls at the end of April, 1915. Traces of fires are visible. The balustrade in the background is the choir of the cathedral whose roof has also collapsed.
(IWM Q 51289)*

Towards a stabilization.

At a time when the road to Ypres seemed open to them the Germans did not appear to make the most of exploiting the breach in the front. Later they will explain the fact by claiming that they had never wanted to pierce the front but simply

This view shows, to the left, Ypres cathedral, severely hit by the bombardment, as it has not only lost its main roof but also those of the nave. By 1918, there will be nothing left of the building. To the right, the empty shell of the Cloth Hall looks even sadder than from the belfry side. The photograph dates from the end of March 1915. (IWM Q 61616)

to test a new weapon, the gas. This is not very convincing, as the battle was going to continue for many weeks and cost thousands of human lives. However, the tests had shown the gas's effectiveness within the first hour of battle. Why, in these conditions, continue the fight so long? And another thing, the use of troops mounted on bicycles and the presence of bridge building engineers showed that the Germans wanted to advance quickly and not content themselves with local success. On the other hand it is difficult to believe that the humble counter-attack launched by the 7th Zouaves was enough to block the Germans. In fact, everything leaves us to believe that the Germans were themselves surprised with the rapidity of their advance and that they did not have a clear idea of the situation on the night of April 22nd. They were probably ignorant of the fact that the whole front line occupied by the 45th Division was wide open and even the Allied High Command itself took some time to realise this. Besides, even though they had failed, the counter-attacks on the hillsides led, on the one hand, by territorials and colonials and, on the other, by the Canadians had certainly worried the Germans in as much as the battles took place at night and total confusion reigned on both sides. Many high ranking German officers even recognised after the battle that, if the winds had

been favourable from the beginning of the day, as planned, the battle would have looked completely different and that the German army would have, without doubt, reached Ypres. It is their failure to take advantage of the situation during the night of April 22nd to 23rd that prevented the Germans from winning a decisive victory. The battle that continued over the following days and weeks would bring no significant modifications to the front line as the Allies were capable of filling in the breach. Over exposed in the east, however, the British were obliged to implement a major fall back.

A rare view of the Cloth Hall taken from the Cathedral square. We notice a group of French liaison officers on the left and British soldiers on the right.
(IWM Q 61615)

One of the first gas masks, a Type P2, distributed to French troops in 1915. The fact that they are wearing Adrian helmets shows that this photograph was taken during the second half of 1915. The very first forms of gas masks appeared as early as April 26th 1915, when General Pellé, in a memo to the armies relates: "In a recent attack the Germans managed to cross our frontline by surprise using suffocating gases: over their trenches formed a sort of yellowy cloud, made of gas heavier than air. This cloud was pushed by the wind on to our trenches, in which the defenders, taken unawares, were put to sleep or suffocated. Large enemy forces, walking behind the cloud, mouths and noses protected by a mask moistened with liquid, managed to reach our reserves without having to fire a single shot (...). It is important to take all necessary precautions to prevent this sort of surprise (...). Alert the troops against a means of attack which, as unforeseen as it may be, is not irresistible. The application over the nose of a handkerchief soaked in hyposulfite caustic soda or simply with water is a way to protect one's self, by and large, against the noxiousness of the gases". (IWM Q 61055)

The Allied losses

The French artillery, placed too close to the front line, suffered considerable losses on April 22nd. The Germans claimed the capture of 52 guns, whilst the French themselves admit

having lost 55. On top of this there were the 29 x 90 mm and 6 x 95 mm guns of the 87 th Territorial Division. The 45th Division lost 16 x 75 mm and 4 x 120 mm guns.

With regard to the infantry, around 1,800 French soldiers were captured by the Germans, of which 200 were severely gassed. Among those who retreated into the French lines, around 600 men were gassed and incapable of fighting again. The number of killed is not known for certain but it is obviously very high: many thousands of deaths. It must be noted that neither General Mordacq, nor the official French history, gives a precise number of French casualties. The Germans only indicated that they captured 1,800 French and 20 British. They did not give numbers for their own losses. On the Canadian side 642 men were taken out of combat (killed, injured, lost, taken prisoner, etc). The map on the following page shows the new frontline of the 2nd battle of Ypres. The German success did not lead to a shift in the balance of power. It was the last German offensive to the west before the launching of the battle of Verdun, on February 21st 1916, ten months later.

This very interesting photograph was taken in May 1915 in the Bois-Grenier sector, France, a few kilometres from Armentieres and so at most 30 kilometres from Steenstraat. These infantrymen of the 2nd Battalion, Argyll and Sutherland Highlanders, had received their masks as early as May 30th 1915, which is less than two weeks after the German attack. These masks are composed of a simple compress, no doubt moistened with hyposulfite caustic soda, and of a pair of glasses. The mask is fastened in a very rudimentary way with a lace or string. These Highlanders wear a protective apron over their kilt. (IWM Q 48951)

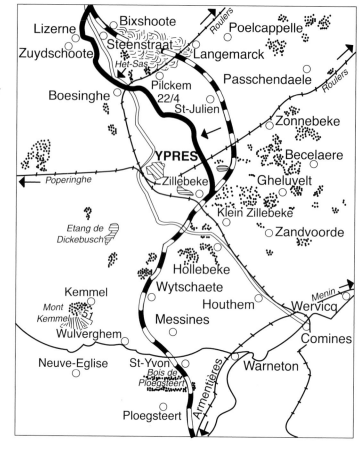

The front line in the Ypres sector during the second battle. The front before April 22nd 1915 is shown as a dotted line. In black, the front line of mid-May 1915. The German advance is notable, but not decisive, and Ypres is still in the hands of the Allies.
(Map: Sandrine Devos © Ysec editions)

Short bibliography

Ducasse, Meyer et Perreux – Vie et mort des Français, 1914-1918- – Hachette, Paris, 1959. 508 pages.

Ministère de la Guerre – Les Armées françaises dans la Grande Guerre, tome II – Paris, Imprimerie Nationale, 1931. 728 pages.

Général Mordacq – Le Drame de l'Yser (la surprise des gaz, avril 1915) – Éditions des portiques, Paris, 1933. 254 pages.

Général Mordacq – Les grandes heures de la guerre. 1915, la guerre des tranchées – Plon, Paris, 1939.

Docteur Nel – Boesinghe ou les combats de la 87e division territoriale sur l'Yser – Coutances.

Claude Prieur – De Dixmude à Nieuport (Journal de campagne d'un officier de fusiliers marins) – Paris, Perrin, 1916. 256 pages.

Reichsarchiv – Der Weltkrieg 1914 bis 1918 : Sommer und Herbst 1915, 8. Band. – Berlin.

Ysec Éditions BP 405
27404 Louviers CEDEX
France
Printed in France
Achevé d'imprimer en avril 2008 sur les presses de Corlet
Imprimeur à Condé-sur-Noireau (14)
Numéro d'imprimeur : 112501